FAITHFUL COLORS

TRINIDEZ MCCOLEN III

Faithful Colors
Copyright © 2021 by Trinidez Mccolen III

All rights reserved. No part of this publication may be reproduced, distributed, or transmitted in any form or by any means, including photocopying, recording, or other electronic or mechanical methods, without the prior written permission of the author, except in the case of brief quotations embodied in critical reviews and certain other non-commercial uses permitted by copyright law.

Tellwell Talent
www.tellwell.ca

ISBN
978-0-2288-3648-3 (Paperback)
978-0-2288-3649-0 (eBook)

TABLE OF CONTENTS

Introduction v

Chapter 1	True love is hard to find	1
Chapter 2	The Tunnel of Temptation	11
Chapter 3	Gold diggers	21
Chapter 4	Keeper	25
Chapter 5	Cheaters Never Win	30
Chapter 6	Loving Her So Deeply	42
Chapter 7	Relationship Goals	51
Chapter 8	My valentine day love	58
Chapter 9	A heart for a heart	66
Chapter 10	A romantic night on me	74
Chapter 11	The lust for her touch	79
Chapter 12	3sum gone wrong	87
Chapter 13	Single and loving it	93
Chapter 14	Faithful colors	98

INTRODUCTION
The Creation of Faithful Colors

One day I just came up with the ideal to write a book on love poems, and I did. I said to myself let me write about sex because people love sex, and the thirst that people have for sex is just crazy. Then I said to myself let me be a little honest about something's, I am writing about.

I had to set my mind on different relationships I been in and out. I had to sit down and think of the love I have lost from women who could have been my one and only, but my stubbing ways wouldn't aloud that.

Faithful color is a book written with excitement, and passion for the lust of love. It is a mysterious book of poems and pleasure associated with love, intimacy, and faithfulness in the mind of one man. It is a humble book with some nice words, and poems that is just sweet and unique. But don't get me wrong are misunderstood because this book does get a little rough ruck it and raw where faithfulness turns to unfaithfulness but grateful with every bite of the fruit.

This is a book with some romantic lustful words, and rhymes that are made to take a women's breathe away if she is the type that love poems are maybe poetry. This book was written with a little ghetto slang kind of talk, so it might be hard for some readers to get clear understanding.

Inside this book there are many different chapters that tell it's on love poems and stories in its own way. They are not all love poems because some of them are very different in a strong opposite way. There are chapters in this book like single and loving it, and then there are chapters like goal diggers and a few more where I stepped out of the love zone.

This book was made out of a love poem in a book call reality check. The title in the book was called loving her deeply. When I wrote the first three chapters they all had lines from the poem loving her deeply put in a different title.

I started it with that love poem and it ended in a different way as I would say. It was pure love and humbleness from beginning to end when I first wrote it. Politeness words of joy with the intense feelings of deep affection.

But then it had a few titles that I thought was a little harsh and I really didn't want to put them inside the book, but I said forget it and added them in. Other than that I just express myself and let myself go to get this book done and completed in a hurry because I was working on something else and my mind was all over the place.

The name faithful color is also a chapter in the book reality check. It was a poem and it was going to be a regular book on things that happen in reality.

Then I changed it to a book with only love poems with some fiction things inside it. I thought that it would be a nice ideal to write every chapter based on some type of intimacy, love and affection inside it.

I started the name faithful colors then I brain stormed for days thinking of some topics to write about. I wanted 14 chapters in the book before I started writing it.

The first three was true love is hard to find- the lust for her touch- and the tunnel of temptation. Then I came up with other title and I said to myself what am I, going to say in these chapters. By brain storming and thinking outside the box I am glad to see that this book is complete.

But I also wrote this book as a movie that I was working on writing, and it was about a man living in the colored community. He is a single man who is all about himself and taking care of his needs into he goes out and finds this beautiful young intelligent lady who made him change his ways. And just like that all of the sudden he is ready to be faithful to that one special lady who he falls in love with.

Faithful colors were going to be a book of love, sex, and addiction, but I made some changes to make it well writing and respectful in a good way. It turned out to be a unique small book of relationship goals, to single goals, and love goals all in one.

While writing this book I had to change my style of writing because I had to be creative in a passionate way. I had to take my mind back in the pass to reminisce on some things I did in and out of my own relationships. I know that I am not a perfect man, and I will never be a perfect man, but I do the best I can to become an even better man then the man that I am. No one can judge me about the things I have done in my pass relationships, but even when chatting with x girlfriends they still try to bring things up and throw it in my face.

It was defiantly something new to me when writing this book because I had to come out with a different approach with the style that I was using to write this book. It's a book with good attention, but it's not made for everyone to read.

When I am writing I always try to write positive things that could bring people some motivation are even some inspiration, but with this I had to go outside the box.

I had to think a little over my limit to put this book together, but I knew that once I got started on it nothing was going to stop me from finishing it.

This book was a change of mind for me, but I wrote it in a different way so I can get it completed fast. Faithful colors was the perfect name for it and it's based on love quotas, relationships and faithfulness plus more.

It got a little fun writing this book and I was laughing underneath my face. I never thought I would let people read this side of me, but its because I enjoyed writing it.

CHAPTER 1

True love is hard to find

Trinidez Mccolen III

There is nothing like finding that true love that your heart desires.

It is like a dream come true to find true love that takes your breath away.

True love that makes you smile can turn into real love that makes you happy.

True love can turn a man into a better man.

True love can open your eyes to better days, and have you faithful in many ways.

True love can take you from here to there like a breath of fresh air.

True love is what every man and woman wants- True love is what we all need.

If you find a love that is true to you, that is a love that is meant for you.

Love will have you so amazed that you will be doing things you never done before.

Love will have some people doing crazy things that they never thought they would do.

What is love if it's not meant for me and you?

Some of us might find true love that will last a life time.

Some of us might never find love in this life time.

But then again some of us might find that true love in a different life time.

There is a special place in all of our hearts where true love really exist.

We chose to love who we want to love and that keeps us dreaming, and wishing for what's next to come.

When you find that true love it puts your mind in a peaceful and graceful place. It's like a magnificent place where all hearts are created.

True love is like a tool that soaks into your heart.

But it is always something when dealing with love, because love can break your heart into little bitty pieces.

Love is real and can reveal as unreal in the end.

The best love I have every find in a relationship started with being friends.

True love comes with loyalty, honesty, and trust built from lust.

A lot of us men search for a love that is humble, sensitive and sweet.

We search for a love to keep.

I can only wonder if I would ever find a love that I can call my own.

A lot of people say that love is blind; I wonder if that's the reason it's so hard to find.

I search for a love that motivates me emotionally.

I search for a love that can help me change my ways and bring me better days.

I search for a love that can sweep me off my feet; I want a love that is brilliant and unique.

I dream of the perfect lady that is made just for me, but in reality that I cannot see.

Then at times I just think and say maybe it's just me- I might have to change my ways.

    True love is hard to find

Maybe I am just to up tight and ambitions about the wrong things.

I know that I'm not a perfect man and I might have let that special lady go in the pass that was all in for me, but my mission is to keep looking forward.

Although I am looking forward I still keep an eye out for lost love that I may have loved and forgotten.

I am getting older and not younger, but as I gotten older I keep my eyes and heart open for that special lady to enter my life to see what my love has to offer.

It seems like time is moving faster and faster, and a lot of people panic when they get older.

They panic because they don't want to be alone.

They panic because they searching for that one person who will just love them only.

I hear it a lot from women time after time; they say things like I need someone just for me because I'm getting to old to be single.

And if you don't committee to them they will walk away and found the next person who will.

He can be a loser, are a killer, maybe a hobo but they don't care long as they got a man lol.

But me being the man that I am, I don't panic when it comes to age. I am proud to be getting older because I do thing much better then when I was younger.

I am ok with my sex game, I love harder and better- my stroke is better plus I am stronger with more energy.

Most importantly my mind is much better.

I am wiser and smarter because back in the day I could just bust out and do something stupid are maybe say something stupid, and be mad at myself for several days.

Now of day I just try to come correct with everything I do and say.

I never push the panic button, and I just stay alert for that special love to enter my life while living my life.

I let the pass be the pass and search for a love that my heart wants.

I search for a love that my heart need, and a love that my heart believes in.

I search for a love that my heart desire.

I search for a love that I can cherish to the end of time.

I search for a love that I can trust.

My search is for true love, real love that money can't buy.

I search the sky, and under the ground, and still that humble love yet to be found.

At times it seems as if I would do anything to find that missing love in my life.

My doors are open and so are my eyes, even though I may come with a disguise but it's just for her to realize.

I know that I will find true love before my time ends. The world spends just to stop and start all over again.

True love goes high above the madness to create happiness.

Maybe were all are blind to real love, but as a man I accept the love that I get from women on a daily because it makes me believe that everyone has someone who is made just for them.

Throughout my life I been in and out of relationships, some were good, and some were bad.

It is sad that they have never lasted. If you ask me a question and say why they didn't last- I would say don't ask.

But life is a challenge and you have to learn from your mistakes. You got to recognize when a relationship is real from one that is fake.

Break ups will come over the smallest things, but sometimes it is one mate pushing the other one away just creating space for one self.

Sometimes good sex keeps a relationship together longer then it supposes to be.

I want a love that's closer than friendship. I want her to give me 50 percent and I will give her 50 percent.

That is something that I've search for in a women sense my younger days. 50/50 makes everything better but, that is hard to find in this life time.

I will search for away just for that day I can say she belongs to me; her love is for me because her loyalty sets me free, as if she has completed me.

I know that I have been blinded by love that entered my life at a young age.

I can remember putting my trust in a young lady and believing that me being faithful to her is the way to be.

That faithfulness in me changed because she wasn't faithful to just me, she had me and another, and in the end I only had a broken heart to show for it.

Love can come back around to me, and I will open my door just for the lust and satisfaction in the sex game.

When I don't have it and I need it, it's like a fruit to my body and it relives a lot of feeling that's been lock inside.

I have grown in many ways and I've learn to play the game the right way by loving women the right way.

I use to dream every day for true love that will make me say, I love you day after day.

True love that makes me says beautiful things, and sings sweet songs from a dream.

I can remember having a big crush on this girl who I lust for so much that she had me doing anything just for her touch.

She had the most beautiful smile and the perfect style.

She was smart with a big heart, and she was kind with the perfect mind.

In the beginning my only wish was for her to be mines.

Yet and still I know that true love is hard to find.

She was sincere, but who's to say if she saw things clear.

She gave me goose bumps whenever she came near.

She made my heart skip a beat, and my love for her was deep because she was so unique.

She was fun to be around; she was smooth romantic and sweet.

This means that she the type that will make a man play the game for keeps.

When she speaks I push repeat because her voice is so soft and sweet.

I never met anyone with her personality and graceful ways.

Her unique style says a lot about who she is as a person; she cared for the smallest things that's how I knew she had big dreams.

But sad to say she was only a once in a life time crush that never felt my touch, and the love I had to offer.

My world goes around and a round, up, down and back around.

From the sky to the ground is where true love should be found.

My heart strives for love and perfection without a blessing.

I have learned a valuable lesson in life when it comes to true love.

Although true love is hard to find, you got to look, listen and grind to find what you want from a lady and what she needs from a man.

I use to walk around with my heart on my shoulders, and I was willing to give it to someone that doesn't see eye to eye with me.

But now today I can look back and say know that's not me because I have changed, but not only have I changed but I have learned.

I have learned not to take love before friendship.

I have learned to take my time and get to know the women before I make a commitment.

I've learned to not take lust for love.

I've learn to be patience and let nature take its course.

I have learned that dreams don't always come true so true love might not exist to me and you.

Most important I have learned to be a man and hold my own and not to live off a female.

I came a long way on my own so before I commit to a woman, I want to be able to hold my own as a man. That's just me and the way that I am.

It is a man job to be the provider and that's what I will do if I committee myself to you.

Don't get me wrong by saying these things because it's not easy out here and now of days it's hard for a man to get his way out here. There is a lot to complain about let's not forget.

But I know that I am a man who strives to be a better man.

I might not be better then the next man, but my love has prepared me for that special someone to enter my life.

Time after time I catch myself thinking about someone who I loved in the pass and the relationship didn't last. Before I even back track my mind do it first.

I think to myself like maybe it's just the thirst, are I am just in the mood for sexually memories.

But once my mind go there then I catch myself shooting a text just to see what she would say, but most of the time when I text she already know what I want.

The conversation starts normal, but one freaky word then get ready for action. As a man you got to be able to back up your talk so my job is to put it down the right way to have her on my line every day.

Everyone go through that faze in one life time where they put they all into a relationship expecting the best out of it, but in the end it's just another down fall.

After that down fall, another search for true love begins.

Some people stop they search after a heart break and just say forget it, I'm better off single.

A heart break can take away from your confidence and have you thinking that there is no out there for you.

You got to stay motivated for love and search even when you are not searching. Although true love is hard to find, keep confidence and in no time you will see that true love is what you have found.

CHAPTER 2

The Tunnel of Temptation

Nothing comes as beautiful as a love poem that floats in the air.

The tunnel of temptation is where the love we share from here to there.

I am a man who has a big heart because my love is deep.

Once I fell in love with a girl who wasn't mines to keep.

She was sweet like a treat, unique and swift on her two feet.

She can take a man heart right out of his chest.

She was one of a kind, but sad to say that she was never mines.

She turned heads when she walked because she knew how to talk that talk.

She had a banging body that will make a man eyes land right on her.

I wanted her so bad, that if she was mines all I would do is brag and brag again and again.

When I first saw her I said to myself that she was the one for me.

I was young at the time and eager for a women's touch.

Looking at her all I seen was the beauty of her smile and her selfish style.

She had me on the tip of her finger and I was willing to do whatever it took for me to be her man.

I was in love with her brown sugar candy looking face, and body without even knowing who she really was.

I can remember telling my friend that this girl is fine as red wine, and I can't seem to get her off of my mind.

One night I went out with a couple of friends for a few drinks and guess who I saw?

Yes it was her Ms. Brown Sugar lol.

I was sitting there shock with my glass of Hennessey and cranberry juice.

A few minutes before my eyes spotter her, I was just laughing and having a good time with the guys.

I mean she took my breath away and I was sitting there speechless.

One of my friends notice it and he said, man isn't that the girl in your dreams? And all the guys started laughing.

I said not the girl in my dreams- she is just someone that I lust for.

So the guys tried to put me up on game, while trying to eager me up to go and start a conversation with her.

I'm sitting there looking all shy and confused without a word in my head to say to her.

After another drink I ask the guys to see was she with a man are is she just posted up with her lady friends.

They say make your move the time is right, she hanging with her buddies.

So here I go heading into the tunnel of temptation.

Here I go being myself the speechless one, but I was feeling a little bit strong and confidence with the liquor in me.

I stood up and walked toward her like she was going to fall in my arms because I was looking fly, and I was smelling fresh saying to myself- I no she can't resist me.

I get to walking toward her trying to make eye contact with her. She looked me in the eyes, and I looked her in her eyes then someone pats me on the shoulder.

I turned around and it was a lady friend from my pass trying to start a whole conversation with me.

I am saying things to try and get her to go away while trying to keep a smile on my face.

Somehow she got me to talk on a subject that through me off balance.

Then I caught myself and realized that I need it to talk to this girl.

10 minute done passed, I looked at her and she was a little tipsy. I see her and her girls was about to leave.

I said to myself oh no! What am I going to do as she was walking away?

In my mind I'm saying to this girl go away go away.

But my time was up and she was headed out the door.

In my mind I was running behind her to stop her and introduce myself, but that didn't happen so I knew that I had to catch her on the rebound.

I finish the conversation with my lady friend and headed back to the table with the guys and they all looked at me like I was a fool and laughed in my face.

I said, it is what it is and maybe I will have better luck next time.

The second time I saw her I looked at her and said how are you doing? And she looked at me like whatever and kept walking.

I saw her plenty times after that and I seem to give up on her because her reaction had my interest in her low.

But once again here I go falling into the tunnel of temptation because she was fine and I was a little bit weak for her.

I can remember the day I approach her and I had a whole attitude, as she was walking I stood in her way so she could look me face to face, and hear what I had to say.

I said to her so you gone just play me like a sucker huh?

She looked at me and said excuse me!

I said so you going to keep ignoring me as I keep throwing my attention at you.

She said what?

So I said; you can't see that I am interested in you?

She said no I just be minding my business.

I introduce myself and told her right away that when she get some free time I will love to take her out.

For a minute she hesitated and was looking like I don't know, but then she said sure we will see what happen.

A week later I seen her and her car was down.

She knew who I was so she smiled at me with the face of attention.

I started a conversation with her and she said she needs transportation to get to work.

Me being me I instantly said to her I got you.

I gave her a ride to work a few times and we had a few good conversation.

Then I started giving her little gifts making her smile. I mean I gave her some nice things especially on valentine day.

I gave her little money to help her out from time to time when I had extra change.

And then one day we hit it off and the stress for her was finally over.

I got her to come to my crib and later on that day she was in my bed.

We smashing, laughing and having fun like we were in love on the run.

I had her in my arms thinking now she is mines. I wasn't trying to be friends I wanted her to be my lady.

I wanted her all for myself, but the whole time it was nothing but a slap in my face.

She played me like a peanut butter and jelly sandwich with no bread on top.

I mean she played me like a fortune cooking with no fortune inside.

I was so in love and I was in it for the long ride.

One minute I'm lost all in my feelings missing her, calling her phone trying to be next to her. Then the next minute I'm in a good sprit loving our space and having fun being alone when she not around.

After a while she got spoil wanting this and that, I mean she wanted more then what a normal girl would ask for.

I told her I am not a baller; I am a working man with a nine to five, all the things you asking for is getting a bit ridiculous.

After I said that, she goes off with this big attitude saying things like, what do I fool with you for if you can't get me what I want.

I guess I said the wrong thing to her because she was a different person after that.

I would take her out and afterwards she would say that she had some other things do.

Yes I was getting worried, and I was confused because she didn't want to spend no time with me in less I had some money for her.

I mean I played the fool before, but this time I felt like a sucker who easily fell in love with the prostitute.

Wow! The tunnel of temptation had me in the tunnel of the lost.

I mean she played her part by tarring up my heart, and I fell for the gold digger who leaves men in a deep tunnel of lost love.

She must have been getting men way before me because she played the game so smooth.

And here I am the good kid who learned to be a thug just to be cool with different faces, getting played like the night entering the day.

At first she was so mysterious and I love everything about her.

Then I found out things that made me fill like a trick and she was my pimp.

All the time I'm thinking I am her number one, but I had found out that I wasn't even her number two, or three.

I went to the bar with some friends to clear my head and to get over her one day.

All of my home boys new what I was going through and one of them said to me, you need to keep your heart in your chest and not in your pocket.

So I'm like what do you mean by that? He said you quick to give your heart to a woman before you truly get to know her.

I couldn't say anything because it was true.

I learned a value lesson not to turn lust into love in less you know for sure that you both love one another.

Sometimes the best love you can get from a person is when you are friends doing beneficial things with one another. That way there is no worries and you both can talk about certain things that don't have one feeling involve.

As they use to say, the best relationship starts with being friends and I wanted more than that.

I think I rushed into trying to be with her without getting to know her personally.

I've been heartless after her, I been keeping my heart out of relationships for years now, and I see things so different because I get to see people true colors.

In the end she wasn't even a friend; my temptations took control of me and made me do unexpected things for her.

My temptation took me from here to there because I wasn't aware.

I was a young man who was willing to give my all for that special lady who I thought would be the love of my life.

This girl seems as if she was speechless, priceless and beautiful, but I found out that wasn't true.

I fell for her in the night, but what's done in the dark always come to the light.

I use think to myself and say how I could have so much lush for this girl that had me in a rush for her love.

This lust I had for her was so real and it seem like she was the one for me because there was no one else there for me at the time.

I notice that my mind took actions without cause.

My heart pause because I willing to give her my all.

Temptation can lead you into a relationship without a purpose.

All relationship must have a purpose are they wouldn't last.

Once upon a time it was all about love and getting to know one another.

But then it ended with greed, separation, and hate for one another.

I came a long way from loving the wrong person the right way, and at times I feel lost for words.

It breaks my sunshine to give my all to someone who gives me less, and bring me more than just stress.

This is why I meditate and focus on reality more than ever, and the tunnel of temptation helps me release my mind and love in different ways.

I have a deep imaging nation so my mind wonders off at times.

Her love floats through my mind leaving me heartless signs.

What we had was once great but in the end it felt so fake- like it was just a mistake.

I am not a perfect man, but I did give her a chance to have me as her one and only man.

I got played and lead on in the wrong way, but now when I see her I have nothing to say.

I use to just walk and talk by letting the tunnel of temptations lead the way.

Now I am ok because I know how to play the game the right way.

CHAPTER 3

Gold diggers

Nothing comes as sneaky as a nibble pluck headed gold digger.

You can give her the world, and all she wants is your money.

You can love her to death and marry her, but her mind is still on your money.

You can be faithfully in love with her, but at the end of the day all she wants is your money.

You can get up every morning and go to work so she can have nice things, but she's a gold digger for away from being a queen.

I let my shoulder lean when it comes to females that scheme.

It is a lot of women out here without the audacity to do the proper things for they self.

I know a lot of women who goals is to hustles a man for what he got.

A gold digger will nibble on you into you have nothing else to give.

When you have nothing else to give then they disappear into the wind.

Females that plot on a man to get them for their money is she really a gold digger, are a hustles?

What really is a goal digger?

Do we consider females who use man for their kids to get child support money as gold diggers.

Is a woman who married to a rich man then divorce him and leave with half of his money are they consider gold diggers.

I mean she came with nothing, but left with everything.

In reality if you erase the man who she has gotten everything from, is it clear that she really has nothing.

How will we adapt to changes as man, and how can we find a woman that loves us for who we are and not for what we got.

How will we see the difference from a gold digger and good women?

I mean we are man and we love our women, but it is a must that we focus on real love because it is some harsh lady's that will break you for all you got if you not up on your game.

I hear it all the time and I see it on social media a lot. I see females saying things like, a man can't get anything free these days but a conversation.

I mean you women really worth that much money? Are is it that you not worth nothing at all.

These days you got to be very careful what you do and say for money because money isn't everything.

Money can get you nice things, but is it real are is it a dream.

The thing with these goal diggers is that man fall quick for them and find they self in a financial dispute.

Now of days you got to be careful who you love because you can end up with more than a broking heart dealing with these gold diggers.

The women that do these things are these the women we consider gold diggers are they just lost women with their mind in the dirt.

Are maybe they just women trying to find their way in life by getting in where they fit in?

I here female yapping about you shouldn't be messing with a man in less he is paying your bills. I am like what? Saying to myself really? What are you talking about?

I myself no that it is a lot of guys out here that are flat up broke, and they don't want to work, but not only that they are loser and user but back to what I was saying.

I mean you a grown women you should have already had your situation under control before that man even came along. So why should he have to pay your bills. Come on now it's all about common-sense.

There is no way that a female should put her responsibility on a man and if she does she probably isn't worth nothing.

A gold digger is a user an abuser to life.

Plain and simple keep your hands off the trigger and stay alert for these gold diggers.

They pretend to be your friend, lover and you're everything, but in the end you will see the lost figures dealing with a gold digger.

I have seen women come in as like they got it all, but they plan is to get you for it all.

Makes you keep your mind on your figures when it comes to these broke nibbling gold diggers.

Always about money, but don't want to work for the money trying to play a man like a dummy silly trigger isn't nothing but a gold digger.

I got cash that I work hard for to provide for my family and you nibble on the winger for some cheese, gold digger please.

They work hard trying to do things right for you, but they only doing it for the money and hoping to break you in the end stay aware my friend.

If you love me, I want you to love me for me, not for the money because money did not make me nor create me.

But who am I to judge because I know I have through some chicks some cash to get what I wanted so really I have no complaints lol. Hahaha

What can I say she finer then fine lol.

Like they say, it isn't tricking if you got it because I got to get mines just in a different way that you get yours.

CHAPTER 4

Keeper

She is a keeper because her love is deeper than the blue sea.

She is like a dream come true to me- when I first met her I fell for her instantly.

I love her and she loves me. Her touch gets me weak because it is her love that I truly seek to keep.

She has a beautiful heart and this I know. She has a beautiful smile that will make the room glow.

She is loyal to me and that's how we grow. I will do anything for her in rain, sleet, even in the snow.

She is a keeper and I am pleased with her life style that is sexy, rough, and wild.

A lot of people sleep on her sexy style that will drive a man wild.

She is the type that makes a man proud because she is trust worthy and sweet- smooth, brilliant, plus she is unique.

She is fine as wine, she is the type that you would wind and dine. Once you see her she will be stuck on your mind.

She has made me change my life because she the type a man would wife.

Her love will turn a boy into a man. I do all that I can to keep her happy in love with me.

She is definitely a sleeper because she is a keeper.

She is humble and sweet, she stands perfectly on her two feet.

She is the type that you would introduce to your mother because she is like bread and butter.

At times I think like there is no one better, like she is in control of the weather.

Let me tell you again that she is a sleeper because she is a keeper.

She is the one for me as you can see, she believes in me and that pushes me to the limit.

I try to do all that I can for her because she has a kind heart.

She is smart and her body is like a work of art. God couldn't have painted a better pitcher; yes she is a sleeper, a granted keeper.

I trust her faithfully because she is blessed gracefully.

She truly is brilliant and unique, in bed she is a freak.

She will do all the things that a man wants from his lady.

She will have you over satisfied like there is nothing that can come between love and pride.

Her love makes my day better no matter the weather. She keeps me in my lain because it's part of game.

She takes my hand because I am her man. I have no plans without her in it.

She is like the beginning and the end. I love her through the thick and the thin.

There is no one sweeter, I am the man beneath her, and most definitely she is a keeper.

When you find that special lady that makes you happy and intense you got to keep her.

If she gives you goose bumps when she is near you got to make sure that everything is clear for her because she is the right one for you.

If she is a keeper you got to keep her close to your heart.

If she loves you and she want to be with you, and you love her but you not ready for relation just yet, then it's your job to do what it takes to keep her in your life.

She does not have to be perfect, but you got to make sure that she will be worth it.

I wake up in the morning next to her feeling like an inspiration in the making because she is mines for the taking.

She makes me fill complete like if I was life great treat.

It is a tremendous feeling to have her in my life because she makes everything right.

I had been through pass relationships where things went up and down.

Times got hard then they got better, then I went from being happy to being sad and unhappy.

We all have our ups and downs in and out of relationship, but nothing is sweeter when you got you a keeper.

It's hard to find that special person that makes you feel complete.

Someone who loves you for you no matter what you are going through.

I am so happy to have this special person in my life because I trust her and lust for her day and night.

She has the right mind, and she is beautiful plus she is finer then fine.

I said it once and I will say it again; it is nothing better than loving the one who loves you.

She makes my life equal simply because she is a keeper.

I never had some one that has me so into them like I am just horny for her love all the time. I can have sex with her for hours and still want more.

When I'm with her there is no score simply because I adore her.

Nothing makes my day go by the right way when I wake up to see her beautiful face.

In the beginning I had to chase for her love, then I had to race for her love. After that I was in a rush for her love.

I wanted her touch and her companionship.

I wanted her for my sexually needs every day in every way.

When I'm feeling relaxed and in a lovable mood I wanted her next to me.

When I am in a passionate mood, I wanted her to be next to me as we sit and sip on some wine and rewind time.

When I'm feeling over worked and stressed out, I want her body to relieve that stress.

When I'm feeling lust, ruff and greedy I wanted to sex her slowly and roughly into she in a deep she sleep next me.

Even though her love is not cheap, but she is mines to keep.

What makes everything perfect about her is that she gives me loyalty support and sex.

I mean she gives me whatever comes next.

She is better than my first, my last and my ex.

Her love leaves me in a deep sleep because she is mines to keep.

CHAPTER 5

Cheaters Never Win

There is always a place to stop just to start all over again from the beginning to the end- cheaters never win.

I am a man and I know that a man is going to be a man to the end, but cheaters never win.

When you in a relationship you can no longer pretend because cheaters will never win.

Being honest is a big thing in a relationship, but then again when you cheat some relationships end. After that you have to start all over again because cheaters never win.

There is a lesson to learn when you are in a relationship. Things can change. Things can stay the same. Things can repeat leaving the mind with no sleep.

When you catch your mate cheating it's hard to let down your guard. You can get away with it if you know how to play your cards, but you got to stay focus to the end because cheaters never win.

I am not a perfect man, but I do understand that cheaters never win.

When you are a couple you got to be strong and you got to block out distraction that will take your mind off the one you love. You got to be that way from beginning to end because cheaters never win.

Maybe in a different life time I will be the perfect man, a faithful man, but then again I play the game to win and I know that cheaters never win.

I can remember my teenage love less years, and my teenage lustful years all in one tear.

I know I had my share of good and bad times from pass relationship.

I know I have been cheated on, and I know that I have cheated when in a relationship.

I have low standers when it comes to my faithful flaws even though I am considered to be a good man.

But no one can judge me for being me because of the gratitude and the goals which I desire.

Growing up I always had this thing for older woman, I liked girls who was more experience and older than me.

I had my share of cake and ice cream lol. I learned a lot from dating older females. I liked older ladies because girls my age weren't interested in me, and the ones that was I was probably to stubbing to be interested in them.

I had a thing for older females because it made me fill like a man when I have full control over a women older than me, and to hear her moan sexually while sexing her made me fill like I was that number 1 dude.

Being young and experiencing that had me feeling like I was the man.

I thought I had game. I was on a mission to love, and my job was to get every woman I had sex with sprung off the D. But that never happen because they came and went like wind as the world spin.

I know I have dated older women who use me just for sex, but who to say that I wasn't doing the same because it's all a part of the sex game.

When I was young I loved so hard with my guard down and one day I paid the price.

I got my heart broken, and got cheated on so I ended the relationship right away with no excuses are question ask. I was cold hearted because I was a good kid.

Latter on down the line I got my heart broking again by someone who I fell in love with.

One moment I'm thinking this girl is all I want and need, feeling pleased at times, but in the end it was another heart break.

I wonder if that is the reason I am the way I am today.

I wonder if I haven't had my heart broken in the pass will I be a faithful man today.

I wonder if I found the right person in the pass will I be a happy married man to day.

I can only wonder was it those heart breaks that made me so independent to be single and conquer on my own.

I wonder was those heartbreaks the reason I am just selfish and lonely in an odd way.

I wonder did my pass relationships teach me a lesson in life not to put my heart first.

I wonder- I can only wonder did my pass hype me up to cheat in my future.

I wonder is it my pass relationship that got me running from being faithful just to one lady.

I wonder if I was a happy married man in a faithful relationship today how would I be.

I wonder will I be happy in every way, but I wouldn't want to be that person if I didn't have anything to say.

I wonder, I wonder a lot because I am a thinker and being a thinker can turn you into a dreamer.

I experience a lot running away from relationships. I wonder is it because I know I will cheat? I know that I have cheated more than once.

It never been about a relationship with me and her, it was about friendship and sex. We had no cemetery; it was all about sex with us.

We sex in the living room, kitchen, rest room, and the shower.

We smashed in the car, in the park just constantly being nasty exploring our sexually abilities.

When I ran into her I knew we were going to smash with any little chance we get.

So here I go telling her about what I got going on, and she telling me what she got going on than come the exchange of numbers.

Right then and there I was thinking of ways to cheat. It's a shame how rude and corrupted the mind works.

I told her my situation and I also told her that I had a new place so she told me to swoop her up like I didn't just tell her I had someone.

We'll let be clear, I said I had a friend, but sooner are later she was going to find out she was more than just that.

But she didn't care and I from my own perspectives I didn't nether.

All the sudden I'm with my lady and I am acting strange and doing unknown things that are getting her upset with me.

I was turning down dates. I was telling her things like I'm chilling to night, I just want relax.

All the while I got this girl on my mind and I am clearly ready to get it in with her.

So one day I and my lady were out having fun and she said she had something to do later on. That quick a bell sounded in my head ring, ring.

I said cool I'm just going to go hang with the family today then chill out and get prepared for work in the morning.

So I'm being sweet, hugging her- then I kiss her and said ok I will talk to you later-love you.

Not even five minutes passed. I hit up the chick and told her what's up, what you got going on. She said nothing much and wanted me to pick her up so we talk and chill.

There was no going out to eat are going to see a movie it was straight one on one talking and chilling at my house.

so I picked her up and we was riding then we headed to my house, I took her inside then went back outside to park my truck in the back which I have no idea why I didn't park it in the garage.

All week we have been talking smack on the phone and texting about what we going to do next time we have sex. On top of that we were talking about making porn in a silly way.

We waste no time in the next 30 min we ripping each other clothes off.

I'm saying to her I have been waiting for this and she like me to. So we jump right at it straight raw like we had no control over our self.

I'm on top hitting it putting it down. Hitting it from the side tossing her over getting it from the back and guess what? We are doing all this with the camera rolling.

So she puts me on the chair and started riding me like crazy.

I'm tipsy off my drink so I drink more so I can last longer without that nut messing up my vibe. I'm having fun. She is having fun. The camera rolling and all the sudden I hear a knock on the door.

Just like that I was like what the cuss word is going on.

My heart dropped because I know I don't have that much company, and don't know one pop up at my house unexpected so I knew something was up.

Then I heard another knock and she like want me to get up.

I'm like dang let me see who this is. I was on rock hard and went soft in 30 seconds.

I walked up to the door and looked through the peep hole. I said to myself oh no! Because it's her, and she yelling out Tyrese I know you in there I see your truck in the back.

I'm standing there heartless, but embarrassed by my own actions and shocked. I did not open the door; neither did I open my mouth.

Ten minute have passed, and she still outside waiting on me to come out.

So she commits to continue knocking and calling my phone. Another five minutes passed so I started thinking that I should open the door.

I open the door and stepped out and she was mad as fire like why you didn't open the door. She said I know you got another girl in there.

So I just went on and came out with it and told her the truth. I said Yes I do I got company.

She like who is she? I said she a friend that I have known for a while.

She said well what's up with me and you, and how you just going to do me like this.

I said I'm sorry I don't know what happen. I made a mistake. She said sorry isn't gone cut it; tell her she got to go.

I told her that I picked her up and I got to take her home.

She stood there and said you know what, do what you got to do I'm not even mad at you and she walked off.

She got in the car, set for a while then texted me and said she better be gone when I get back and pulled off.

I was surprise in a way because she didn't get out of control; she just let me know that she knew that I was up to something.

She was older mature and grown so she didn't play the mind games because she had a lot going for herself.

She had a big house that she owned; she had cars, money and kids that she had to take care of so she never let herself get out of control.

Weeks later we were still messing around despite my cheating, but we was slowly evaporating from one another.

Then it got to the point where I would only see her maybe twice a month, we was spinning less time together.

We weren't together anymore, but she had accepted my ways and still hung out with me from time to time. The kind of hanging out we did was having sex.

Into one day she told me that she had a male friend who wanted a relationship with her, and they planned on making a commitment to one another.

I was happy for her and I told her that. I also said to her that I hope he treats you better than I did.

She went about her way and I went about mines.

From the beginning to the end, bad decision will make you start all over again because cheaters never win.

I know that I may have lost a good woman who was a good person, but most important I lost a good friend because cheaters never win.

Throughout my years I have learned to adjust because at the end of the day, I know that it is all about me and my decision making.

I know that I cheated and it's a fact that I cheated more than once. So I may have lost the game and learned a lesson in relationships.

Let me tell you a story, a true one at that. I was in a relationship once before when I was around 26 years of age. I was in a relationship with a 41 year old woman.

She was cool, friendly, kind and strong with a big heart. I was young kind, but heartless with the world on my shoulder and not caring at all, but I was graceful and blessed.

I met her at a gas station and I guess she had a thing for young men because after a little conversation and a little 411(information) I ask for her number and she gave it to me, then it was on from there on out.

The relationship was smooth going in the beginning and she was nice to be around on a chill kind of a day.

Being with her gave me great feelings and I would do anything for her at the time. I had gone through some things and I also learned some new things because we got closer after a couple months went by.

She had been telling me that she wanted me to meet her kids, and I would say cool, but it took a while for that. So one day out of the blue with nothing particular going on she invites me over to a BBQ. (Barbecue)

It was crazy and shocking in the beginning because her kids were nearly my age and I was like wow! But everything was cool, we drunk and talked a little sports are whatever was going on in the streets.

It was a smooth going process and a learning process for me being a young man dating a lady with kids close to my age.

I was young and everything I had, I worked for it. I had my own house and car at a young age.

I was working on being independent, but I was still struggling in reality.

Before I bought my house I lived in a one bed room apartment for 5 years.

The day I moved I was so happy to get away from there and when I did it seem like everything had changed for me.

Being at my old spot I couldn't even sleep at night because someone is always out trying to steal cars are whatever. So it was a blessing just to get away from those East St Louis areas. But back to the story I invited her to my house and she would stay a night with me a lot.

I know that I had my share of problems and when my car was down, I didn't have any transportation and she would pick me up and take me around.

She would get me from point a two point b and I was thankful to have her in my life at that particular time.

I would do a lot for her and she would also do a lot for me, but not only that, she used to spoil me and I wasn't up for that.

I know a lot of man want they female to give them money and buy them clothes, but that wasn't my style because I can do those things for myself.

She used to get me things for the house like bathroom sets, kitchen table cloths, and I was ok with that.

She used to get me clothes, like shirts and pans and then I'm like oh wow you don't have to.

Then she even bought me some boxer drawers and I'm like now you going to for. lol.

I guess I was putting the D down right because she got extra close where I'm like (OMG) do I need to create some space.

With crazy thoughts running through my head everything was smooth going. I had no worries about our relationship because I didn't have anyone in my life at the time.

But I did have a few female friends on the side but they weren't important at the time.

One day I ran into a female friend of mine who I knew when I was in my apartment. I knew that I was going to fall for her in a relationship are not because all we use to do is smash (sex) we use to smash for hour constantly getting it in.

CHAPTER 6

Loving Her So Deeply

She equals me and we equal us together we lust and never fuss.

She has always been there for me when my spirit needs a lift.

She is like an extraordinary gift that I seek to keep.

The love she has for me sweeps me off my feet.

She is like a child hood crush that got me deeply in love.

Faithful Colors

She is mine; she is mines, I am happy to say that time after time.

Every time I sip some wine she takes my mine in time.

In time real love is what I have found from the sky to the grown.

She is like my strength when I am weak.

Her voice is like magic when she speaks.

Sometimes she makes me rush just for her touch.

She is my pride -She is my lover, I don't think I would ever find another.

Loving her deeply, Keeping her secretly.

I give her my trust and she gives me honesty-together we are a dynasty.

In her eyes I see us forever lasting from passion and love.

I can promise her the world and still see that she deserve more.

For you my love I will open up doors because you are someone I simply adore.

No matter what you do my heart will always be true because I am deeply in love with you.

I cherish her heart and keep it in a safe place. I don't think that her love can ever be replaced.

Her beauty is priceless; she gives me strength and righteousness.

She make my life seem complete, she is a treat, a gift that I plan to keep.

In the beginning it was only me-then it became us all the sudden her love had me in a rush.

I had to earn her trust so I dedicated my time on writing her love lines.

In the beginning I was feeling blind because her love is what I had to find.

Without a doubt I knew that she would be mine only if I gave it more time, because in time she is mine.

My love for her is deep, deeper then sleep, so deep that I will never cheat.

Loving her deeply to the end of my time

She is finer then fine and prettier than most- she is beautiful from far away and up close.

Loving her deeply; through thick and thin, she is my angle and my best friend.

Real love last forever, through the stormy weather and difficult times we come together because her love was meant to be mines.

Beautiful days leave us with emotion and devotion. From the high to the low, real love will show and grow as the time go, and this I do I know

She is like the stars in the sky and I am the moon that sits up high.

Above is our love- below we grow and build trust from the lust as we crave one another.

Her sweetness gets my attention at all times; she is like poetry to my mind.

She has this style that I can explain, that makes a man stay in his lane.

Loving her deeply all the time, how I still can't believe how pretty she were the first time I laid my eyes on her.

I was surprise, and all eyes were on her, but really my eyes were the only one on her.

She had me on a string looking like she was an angle without wings.

She takes my breath away, and I am in love with the feeling of loving her every day.

It is amazing how our love grew from hugs and kisses, all of the sudden were sexing even in the kitchen.

Our love started slowly and grew bigger and deeper than before.

Our hearts connect like we were made for one another.

Her amazing touch has lifted me off my feet now only her love I seek.

I must say that it is an intense feeling of deep affection the way me and this lady connect.

First it was lust then it was love, then it was us cherishing our love.

Memories of the pass made us laugh in the future and it seems as if all the bad times made us closer, stronger, wiser, companion to do the right things that would make our love last.

There is nothing like her tenderness that fulfills my deepest thoughts.

She gives me emotion with a deep vibe that grooves me to a love song without a beat.

Our intimacy is like a deep affection that calls my name in the middle of the night to wake me up to sleep again, just to show how deeply in love we are in.

Loving her deeply to the time expires, she is like electricity and I am the wires.

Beautiful like the morning sky, she is to me. I love her and she loves me.

What I see she see, there is nothing like the love she gives to me.

She is like faith and I have faith in our love, which is deep. I plan to keep and treat her with the proper respect that she deserves.

Never ask why because there is no question why I love her so deeply.

Loving her deeply and keeping her secretly

I am in love with her smile, and her unique style that separate her from others.

She cook and clean, but what I like the most is when she sing and make the humming birds sing songs of a sweet dream that makes the bells ring.

Loving her deeply with my heart and giving her all my trust without a fuss.

Together it is us keeping our love going around and around through the ups and the downs.

I still can remember the day I met her, she was so pretty that I didn't have it in me to speak right away.

I was loss for words and I had to think before I spoke.

For a moment I thought I was in a dream, but clearly I was a wake and my eyes were stuck on her as if I was hepatize by her beauty.

Her style was unique and her voice was soft and sweet, she was like a gift.

She was like a treat to me, and someone I plan to never let go, someone I live to keep.

I love her deep because she is sweet, perfect and smart with big heart.

Her passion is deep and I love everything about her because she is a strong minded lady who has everything going right for herself.

She has pride and she is a faithful believer in only God.

She is independent, but I give her my hand whenever it is need it.

I can remember one Sunday morning I saw her walking in the grocery store. This was the second time that I saw her, I said to her you are beautiful with a perfect body, you are what every man wants.

She looked at me and smiled and said why thank you for the compliment.

I said to her I really mean that. The whole time I was thinking that she is too much for me, but I was wrong because we had a good conversation, and started a little friendship thing after the conversation.

At times I would try my luck and it wasn't easy as she played the hard to get roll.

She stood like a lady that I have never seen but in my dream, and in my dream she was over everything.

There is a special place inside of her heart that only the right one can reach. That special place in her heart only accepts love.

I am in love with her briefly and deeply.

In the mist of love like a one hundred year old toad follow me down this road where stories get told and knowledge get unfold.

I can't believe how deeply I am in love with her.

She will turn a man night into day in a beautiful way, just to wake up and see her face.

We started on the down low and now our love goes high above the stars.

Constantly making love to her has gotten me weak for her touch.

How could I fall so deep in love?

I catch myself thinking of her day and night asking myself question time after time.

Does she love me the way that I love her?

Are we meant to be like to love birds in the tree?

She is like an angel without the wings.

She makes me sing sweet songs from a dream.

She is everything to me- my love-my life-my wife and my queen.

I open my eyes and I see her on my TV screen.

I will adore her always because she is sincere with a good heart.

She is smart, kind and fine.

She uses her mind and she is always on time.

She stands tall and she is proud of herself for what she has accomplished.

When we together somehow she always spark up a good conversation with me.

It is amazing how much love she brings to the table.

When I am not able she is, and when she not able I am.

When I am not able, she do for me the same as I do for her

We are like a match made to be together.

When there is bad weather we are together making everything better.

At night we walk and talk about the future and what we plan to accomplish together.

She brings out the honesty in me like she is the key to my mind in time.

One day she made me realize that her love is what got me on the right path when I was living in the aftermath.

Loving her deeply for who she is to me.

Her beauty and soft well-spoken voice give me no choice but to fall for her only to stand tall for her.

She is like a source of power without a force.

Her loyalty and kindness is not to be taking for a weakness.

She is sweet like a treat and she is mine to keep.

She is like a beautiful heart, that no one can break are remake.

She is like the sky, that no one can take are make.

There is love- there is hate- she is above my every mistake.

From known and back then she is still part of me and she still is my best friend.

There is nothing like having someone special in your life.

I am in love with her so deeply, morning, noon, and night.

We never fight because we talk to make things right.

I can say a million things to make her feel special in one day because she is beautiful in every way.

There will always be someone you will love and cherish with all of your heart. Together we are like a symbol that last forever and ever. No matter the weather in the end we will still be together.

CHAPTER 7

Relationship Goals

There is nothing better than a relationship when you love someone with all of your heart. If you love someone who loves you and the both of you are willing to make that commitment, then the best thing to do is make it happen and let the magic begin.

When you and your partner both are on the same page it makes the magic happen faster, and it puts an every lasting love into the relationship.

Love is a four later word, but it is a big word that is hard for a lot of people to say to their mate are maybe a love one.

When it comes to love when in a relationship, it is a sensational thing for two mates to be deeply in love physically, emotionally, sexually and faithfully.

When a couple is faithfully in love with one another that is the pride of being in a relationship. The pride you get from a relationship brings a family together as one.

Some people are end and out of relationships because they can't handle the pressure, are they might have they own personal reason to be free from a relationship.

It's a lot going on and not a lot of folks are compatible being in a relationship because they relationship goals might be different. They might have solo goals and they might be peaceful living alone preoccupied by they self-made accomplishments.

Many couple have goals that they plan to accomplish while being together, and some couples have no goals but still they stay together as one living to be as one.

Most relationships last a life time; those are the ones who believe in one another no matter what they do, are may have been through.

Some relationships don't last at all, and they end so fast that it seem like it was just a waste of time. A relationship can start, and three months later you can see the finish line where the relationship ends.

A lot of individuals will find that everlasting love in a relationship, and some of us will be searching for a life time just to find someone who loves us for who we are.

When you and your partner have good relationship goals, there is a lot that can be accomplished between the two. This will be the tip off the head in the starting of everlasting love.

Love is brilliant and unique, smooth gentle plus sweet.

Every man and women search for a love that they can call they own. When they find that love they both can stand like a king and queen in their own zone.

A lot of people search for a relationship that will last a lifetime but it is like a dream because that kind of relationship is hard to find.

We can search here and there; we can start a relationship and end it for a new relationship that is even worse than the last one.

Sometimes it be like a learning process, and you just got to keep focus and pray that God send the right one your way.

Most of the time people in and out of relationships just to realize that they better of being single.

I think a lot of people get caught up in the sex game because the sex can be so fire, (good) but they never realize that there is no chemistry between the two.

Yet and still they try the relationship and it don't last because they minds are on two different pages.

One of the most importing relationship goals is being able to communicate with your partner. If there is no communication between you and your partner the relationship will start and finish fasters then then the wind as the world spin.

When you and your partner have good communication skills between the two you can make a bad relationship last for years because the two is in love with the conversation and understanding that they both share.

The sex can be bad the food they cook can be terrible, but the relationship can be moving in slow motion because they share a great conversation.

The communication they have can put extra time on to their relationship, but it's bound to end sooner are later because of the missing pieces they don't have to make it a complete relationship.

A lot of people fail to realize that when you communicate you salve problems.

Communication is a problem saver, when it comes to a relationship that is falling apart. And even if the relationship is falling apart by communicating you can get a lot of things understood.

Without communication you can get a lot of things miss understood.

One partner can be thinking one way and the other partner can be thinking a different way. When there is no communication there is no understanding, and when there is no understanding there is no reason for the relationship to continue.

It's a lot of relationships that last a life time because the two have good chemistry and they know how to communicate when one do something wrong are they both don't disagree with one another.

When it comes to communication everything is right and that is a relationship goal made for two people who love one another no matter what.

Today we live in a world where a lot of relationships are based on sex.

Sex can contribute a lot in a relationship because it sets the mood when you got too many worries, and can't seem to get your mind set on the right things.

Me personally I think that sex is a big part of a relationship because it is some men and women has come of custom to do to time.

Sex is like fruit to our bodies and it can help the relationship in many different ways.

I have heard people say to me that sex is not a relationship goal, but in our young minds I still say that it truly is.

One partner can want it as bad as the other and it's not sad to say it, but if they can't get it from their mate they will go find it elsewhere.

Sex can help in many ways and I know this for sure. Sex can help you sleep better at night especially when your partner is lying next to you afterwards.

Sex helps relieve the stress when you got a lot going on and can't seem to focus on what to do.

Sex can relieve the mind and give you a better understanding on a lot of things because after sex you will be more relaxed.

Sex can motivate you intentionally and emotionally. Sex will have you in a good mood on a bad day.

If the sex is right the relationship can seem right because the two partners are infatuated with the sex that they constantly have that makes them seem as one.

Another relationship goal is to trust your mate and be honest no matter what. I know a lot of people say that being honest only brings more drama because you tell them the truth and the truth will only start another argument.

Some say that it's better not to say a word and let it pass over for the relationship can stay peaceful.

Trust and honesty is the key to a healthy relationship.

When you can trust your mate through the thick, then you can manage to trust them when things are thin.

When you and your mate trust one another there are only good things a head for you both.

With trust the relationship is more compatible and steady. And honest comes with trust so that just make everything perfect in a lovably way.

When a relationship is built on trust you can find real love, and trust only open doors to new life and new things in a valuable relationship.

Being honest is like taking a chance at trusting your partner to be faithful, loveable and happy in love to the end of time.

It is a fact that honesty is a tool for love and it is growth to the roots of the relationship.

Trust can build a strong foundation in a relationship that can lead to marriage. Marriage is the final solution to an honest and trustworthy relationship.

Generally we all know and understand that a healthy relationship can turn into marriage and that is when two people make public pledge or commitment to live together and share their lives in a way that is recognized legally, socially and sometimes religiously.

Being able to travel together is a big thing when it comes to relationship goals. When you are able to sit and talk with your mate on a long road trip, I think that would spark up some good thoughts and end it with some good stories are maybe better memories.

There is nothing like having fun and memories with someone you love.

Road trips are a flight through the sky will be the perfect thing to do when in a relationship.

I know a lot of man will rather chill lay back and do some things around the house, but there is a time when a man has to step up and take that trip to better his own relationship.

The trip can lead to something better later down the line. It can bring more smiles into the relationship and when there are smiles in the relationship there is happiness.

Most people say a couple that travel together stay together. And they have more sexually desire for one another. It can cut the stress in half and form a better romantic mood.

The most important thing about a relationship is to be very close with your partner in a friendship way. Being best friend and not just romantic partners is like the solution to a perfect relationship.

A relationship that starts as friends is a relationship that sometimes last the longest. Friendship can sometimes makes the love last longer because the two have a better bound.

CHAPTER 8

My valentine day love

There is nothing better than giving that special someone your love and comfort on a special day.

I can remember it like yesterday, she was the lost love in my life, and I enter her life with my heart on my shoulders.

This girl was younger than me and beautiful as the day.

She was sweet like a treat and she was mines to keep.

Her love swept me off my feet because she was so beautiful and unique.

I was lost into she came in my life and gave me a chance at love.

The passion we had was so exciting and exclusive.

The love making was rough and passionate.

Then on other days it was slow and smooth.

She was my gal and I was her guy, but not always do we see eye to eye.

She was like a treasure from above, and on this day she became valentine love.

Her beauty expressed poet in a way like no other and her name was poetry.

She was fine and one of a kind, like a gift- the most expensive wine.

She was the first in line when anything came on my mind.

She makes me want to rewind time just to find her love that had me blind.

She makes me say wow I am so thankful that she is my valentine.

When we next to each other, it's like no one can get our minds off one another.

She is smart, wise and just seem so perfect in every way.

She turns my night into day, just to see her walk away takes my breath away.

When we away from one another for days, we come together like birds flying south for better weather.

She is clever and her mind is on another lever.

She makes my heart sing sweet song on and on again.

There is nothing better than love when it comes to my valentine queen.

I dream of us doing wonderful things that last a life time.

Now of days it's so hard to find a girl with the right mind.

Time after time she stays on my mind.

She is my valentine and she is fine.

We go on dates on late nights and that keeps our vibe at ease.

She gives me good love that makes me act right.

I pray and say thank you God for this day because I want my love to fill special on this Valentine's Day.

My boo is beautiful in every way, and she deserve the best gifts on Valentine's Day.

She is my bae and I love to see her face every day.

What can I say; I never had a girl that loves me this way.

She puts a smile on my face and she has me thankful in every way.

Through thick and thin she is my angle and my best friend.

I can only wonder will our love last forever, even though the stormy weather.

Even through difficult times we come together like love that was meant to be.

Once I stood alone just me being me, but when she came into my life she has completed me.

My valentine love welcomes me with open arms.

Her body is warm, soft and comfy.

I love being next to her, she tells me that I bring out the best in her.

She is the kind of girl that makes you play the game for keeps.

Beautiful days leave us with emotion and devotion.

From up high to down below, our love show and it will constantly grow as the time go, and this I do I know.

She is like the stars in the sky and I am the moon that sits up high in the sky.

Above is our love-below we grow and build trust from the lust as we crave one another.

She is a sweetheart and she gets my attention at all the time because she is like poetry to my mind.

I am in love with her deeply because she has a special place in my heart.

I still can't believe how pretty she was the first time I laid my eyes on her.

She was dressed in all white and she had every man eye site.

She was the friendly type, and didn't have any stuck up ways, but she knew how to play the game right.

She was a young lady with her head on her shoulders.

She wasn't up tight, but she was kind of mean in a pretty way.

I step to her, and she welcome my conversation, then I said some things that made her smile.

I ask was she single and she said yes in a smart kind of way.

I ask for her number and she denied me that.

I ask her out on a date and she denied me that as well.

So I ask her to be my valentine in a playful way, and she said sure why not and laughed out loud.

So I let go that day and she said well if you see me again and I'm still single your wish might come true.

I look at her and said wow! It's like that? Ok my valentine

She said yes indeed and walked away looking like a beautiful UN wrapped gift.

I stood there looking like I was in zone 3. Saying to myself, man if she was mines I will be playing the game for keeps.

I saw her again and said what's up, and she smiled and said not you again.

I said wow! Really is you always this difficult?

I said to her you should already know what I want Ms. Valentine.

Thinking in my head saying omg poetry is so fine looking like one of a kind.

Then I said to her, this time I'm not even gone ask you on a date, I just want you to hook me up you no.

What's the 411 on you so I can know the right things to say to make you smile?

For a matter of fact tell me where you gone be so I can be there to.

If you going to the grocery store, let me no because I want to be in the same line with you.

If you going to church let me no so I can be at the same church with you. I just want to see you again, and I promise I want even talk to you no more if you are not interested.

Then I said -You know what you just name the place and I will be there.

So she told me she was going jogging Saturday morning and if I was a no show don't bother her every again.

Man I was up out and about that morning lol I was there before she even showed up, standing there like are you ready for this.

She smile at me once again and said you just as strange as they come and laughed out loud.

But we hit it off that morning and been on the same page every sense.

I gave her the most beautiful flower that smelled like the beauty of life.

I had Ms. Valentine on my line and let me tell you this, she was worth every flower and deserved more by the hour.

She can brighten up a man's day with every word she says.

She takes my breath away and I am in love with the feeling of loving her every day.

It amazes me how love can grow once you get to know a person on the inside.

Our love started slowly and grew bigger as our minds connected, and then it seems as if we were just made for one another.

Everyone dream of finding that special someone who will make their life better. Most of us will find that one person who will make the dream and search for love stop.

Sometimes you will settle for what you got, but inside you might be wishing that person could fulfill the needs of the person who makes all your dreams come true.

I must say that it is an intense feeling of deep affection the way me and Ms. Valentine connected.

There is nothing that I regret about her love, six answers and the answer is all the above.

Loving her deeply and keeping her safely in my arms was the plan I had in hand.

She the type that a man will spoil and do anything to keep.

Once you had a taste of her love you will be whipped and your life will be incomplete.

You will be a loss for words into she is yours to keep.

Briefly I speck words that reach her heart to observe a better communication between us.

She is my valentine created in a time where we give our all just to fall in love with that special someone who makes us smile.

There is always that special someone who we will trust with all of our heart.

She is like pride to my joy, loving her in the beginning has giving me a perfect ending.

My valentine love has gotten me all warm up and charming to do things to keep her happy.

She is like no other; she is my lover, partner and friend to the end.

I cherish our time so it can last in time.

I love her for a life time not just on valentine day.

I love her for who she is and not for what she do are say.

But hey today is Valentine's Day and I want my bae to feel special in every way.

It is nothing better than love when you can say you have a love to call your own.

It is a great feelings I get from loving the right person who loves me the way I love them.

I think about our sensational thoughts connecting and that moves our love higher than normal.

When our emotion get involves that's when the love gets stronger, and once the love is stronger nothing can break that special vibe.

Ms. Valentine has made Valentine's Day become so special to me because I can make the one I love feel special on this day which is not her birth day.

So every year I try to get in the valentine mood to make my special lady smile and say I love you.

CHAPTER 9

A heart for a heart

Loyalty is proving to be one of the most important things in a relationship.

Then there is communication because communicating with your partner is important.

Then there is trust and honest, a relationship cannot continue without trust and honest and that's a fact.

You also have forgiveness. Even though there are certain things that are hard to forgive.

Me personally I feel that Forgiveness is extremely important in a relationship.

Then you have respect, respect is the foundation of a healthy relationship because how can you disrespect the one you love and care for.

There is also appreciation. You got to appreciate your partner for who they are and acknowledge the things they do just for you.

In a relationship you got to be supportive emotionally. Both partner got to be supportive of one another to make the bound stronger.

Happiness is important in a relationship because if the two partners are not happy then the relationship is bound to end.

It's all about a heart for a heart in a relationship

Most relationships are about give and take, and when one partner only takes and never gives something is bound to break.

These days when in you are in a relationship you got to have an open heart and learn to accept certain things the way they come.

But what is a relationship without the hearts that connect to one another?

When two hearts come together as one, it is a sensation feeling.

There is nothing better when two partners connect with their mind, body and soul.

When to hearts come together as one it's like life great treat feeling of satisfaction.

Nothing is better than love when it comes from the heart.

You can say you love someone easily, but the question is do you mean it.

When push comes to shove it's all about proving your love to that special person whom you love so much.

Sometimes proving that love to that special person is not easy as it may seem.

You can show your love in many ways and the person you love so much want even get it are understand in the beginning.

I have a big heart and my love is deep.

My heart don't speck, but it give me special feeling that be having me willing to give my all to fall in love with the heart that I desire the most.

A heart for a heart can brighten up my day in the best way.

True love comes from the heart because it is within the heart.

It takes two hearts to make one, love comes and love goes, but real love can live in your heart forever.

You can love someone and separate from that person, and end the relationship, but inside your heart you will still have a place in your heart for that person you once loved.

Every man and women search for that one true love that they heart desire.

A heart filled with trust is an honest heart; an honest heart tends to be a blessed heart.

A blessed heart is a heart that cares.

Ask yourself what is a heart without a heart that loves you?

What is a heart full with hate? Is that heart a mistake?

What is a heart full of love? Is that a heart from above?

What is the definition of love without a heart that gives u feelings?

What is the definition of a relationship if the two hearts can't come together and create one?

There is no life without a heart.

A heart is one of the main parts of our body.

We all need our hearts to love, live, and give.

Two hearts that love one another can create a beautiful thing.

A heart starts with love and trust from the wound all too soon.

The heart is like the moon to this world; it's bigger than the stars and means more then everything around it.

The heart does not dream are see anything, but it feels and live us eternally.

My heart gives me feeling that no one can explain, but I search for a love that will truly complete me.

My heart is filled with compassion and many times in my pass relationships I tried putting myself in my partner shoes to make things work.

At times I would believe that a lack of problems gave me the ability to keep things in perspective.

I use to anticipate doing things that helped me avoid problems because I thought it was the key to a happy relationship.

It's like this; if I comment myself to someone and they give me they heart then it's my job to give my heart to anticipate the starting of a new companionship.

This is what a heart for a heart is 50/50 in a relationship.

And if I give you a hundred percent of me, and you give me a hundred percent of you then we both should be on the same page.

It's just the simple fact that when both mates give a hundred percent the relationship last longer.

The relationship is stronger and stronger is better.

A lot of us man tend to hide our love and trust.

We cover our hearts and sometimes that keeps us strong.

But some hearts are made to be broking Just to be fixed.

A fixed heart is a stronger heart then a broken heart.

A heart that has been broking supposed to make better decision.

The broken heart supposed to be smarter and wiser.

It supposed to be smarter and wiser because it been through some things, and it had time to learn from its own mistakes.

The broking heart doesn't fall for to many things as that the unbroken heart fall for, but who is to say.

My heart is pure, but it has been broken.

I catch myself hoping for the best of things but they never come.

I accept the broking heart I had in the pass because it has made me a different man inside.

I have walked the walk, and talked the talk. That walk and talk taught me a valuable lesson in life.

Always remember that the heart is blind so never let it lead you.

The heart can give the mind love signs even though it is blind.

A new heart is filled with love, joy, and happiness.

A heart for a heart also means love and satisfaction between to partners.

I am a man in action and my heart desire the most.

I wonder will my heart ever find the girl that deserves the most.

If she is interested in me she has my sympathy.

If she is amazing, she want be easy for me to please.

If she isn't amazing, I can give her the world and she still want be pleased.

If she is worth it I will give her my time, and cherish her like she is mines.

She will be the love of my life from the beginning to the end.

If she is not worth it, I will step back and let nature take its course.

If I fill that I have a chance, I want give up on her.

If I do give up on her it's because she wasn't worth my time.

If she is special I will love her to the end of time.

If she is not then she will be someone who came, went and I forgot.

If she is smart she will welcome my heart, and my every conversation.

If she isn't smart, she probably would ignore me and go her own way.

If she is meant for me then it is only right for me to get on one knee and make that commitment.

I can only wonder how far is my heart willing to go for love and all the beautiful things that come with it.

Sometimes I wonder if I should hide my honesty and cover my heart just to protect it from getting broken again.

I wonder will she be the one who brings out the best in me are will she be like the others only here to bring out the stress in me.

Trust give the heart signs that, everybody going to hurt you.

So sometimes it is mandatory that you keep up your guard no matter what.

But life is all about changes and chances, without changes and chances everything will be stuck the same.

A beautiful rose will brighten up the sun shine.

In the nick of time true love is what you will find.

What is a heart if it isn't mines?

If the heart is blind is love blind to?

These are just some little rhyme made for me and you.

Cover your heart with your pride and live your life to the fullest because real love is valuable to your hearts.

It takes two hearts to make one heart.

Together these hearts are magnificent from start to finish.

Every man and women will desire love once they heart catch feelings.

I do believe that a lady can bring out the best in a man, and that's what a man needs.

A lot of man doesn't see real women these days beside they mother, and that's who bring out the best in them.

You got to learn about self-motivation so you can learn to push for greatest from within.

There is nothing that can brighten up the day like a heart filled with pride.

A heart that is true and alive is a heart that has been blessed by God

A heart for a heart -a good heart comes in disguise.

A heart in search for love is a heart filled with lust.

When you have open eyes, and an open mind you can find love in no time.

CHAPTER 10

A romantic night on me

I am blessed to see all that I can see, but for you my dear this is a romantic night on me.

You are so special to me that on this night you are the only one I wish to see.

I am in love with the feeling of loving you morning, noon, and night.

When I am feeling down one kiss from you and I am alright.

You always brighten up my day in a beautiful way.

You are gorgeous to me no matter what anyone has to say.

I am proud to say that you have brightened up my night in a magnificent way.

It is pure sensational when you have someone that make you do and say sweet things.

I mean she has a graceful body and she is beautiful inside and out without a doubt.

She is so special to me and that is why I give her my love gracefully.

This night was made just for her and eye, and that's no lie.

She has the best lips as we tongue kiss under the moon light.

I search for higher heights on romantic nights.

I love keeping her warm in my arms doing the storm.

She is my right when I am wrong; she is my strength that makes me strong.

She keeps me going when I am feeling down like a king with no crown.

Together we search for peace in the middle east.

What's done in the dark always come to light, but there is nothing better than a romantic night under the moon light.

On a beautiful night filled with passion and desire, we live in a time zone where time never expires.

It is sensational for a man when he loves someone and does all that he can to please the women he love.

There is nothing better than romance when it enhance the passion into a relationship.

One day I set to myself thinking of some Romanic things to do for the one I love.

So I planned a romantic night like a summer flight under the moon light.

I was felling tense and emotional all the while I had this lust for her touch.

I had rented out a room with the Jacuzzi and bubble bath waiting for her.

The night was young and the day was perfect. Just by looking at her you would know that she is worth it.

I had sexy rose puddle all over the bed, and some red wine with some dom perignon.

I order us a dinner, we had baked stake, broccoli, mac and cheese with some mash potatoes and gravy.

It was about to be a night we will never forget because it was about to go down.

I had got her a gift and it was a beautiful necklace with a heart charm on it to show a symbol of my love.

I called her and told her that I missed her, then I said, I'm ready everything just waiting on you.

She said she was already on her way.

When she came in she was surprise because she never seen this side of me before.

Everything was beautiful, the lights were deemed and the room was filled with sexy colors.

She was all in her feeling, but she was shock and confused about me, and who I was at the time because she saw a different side of me.

She had been on my mind for a while and I was in need of her loving.

We ate good set and talked about what every came on our minds which made the mood fascinating and perfect.

After the food and conversation we jump in the Jacuzzi and relaxed our bodies then we jumped in the bubble bath.

I started rubbing her down giving her a good rub in the tube. I couldn't wait to get her in the bed for the sex to start.

But how things were going in the bubble bath, I knew we weren't going to make it to the room before sexing.

I felt her goose bumps as I starting kissing on her neck with my hands all over her body. Before you know it I was up inside her giving her the D in the tube.

It was passionate and like an emotional roller coaster. We were both feeling each other on this romantic night on me.

I picked her up and dried her off then carry her to the bed room to finish what we started.

I gave her the ruff love making sensation in bed which is how she liked it.

She said to me, I love you and no one never done this to me before.

I knew I had her under my control and she was indeed to be mines.

When my heart is drilling and craving that special lady who means the world to me, I will do almost anything to get her in bed to fulfill the both of our needs at ease.

It is a must that I do anything to please the one I love sexually, mentally emotionally by any means necessary.

I swear it seem like when you do good things for good people blessing just come at the door, but when you do good things for the wrong people you can see yourself falling down.

I do what is best for this lady daily and everything is on me romantically.

CHAPTER 11

The lust for her touch

I lust for her touch because she is one of a kind with the perfect mind.

She is so fine that when she leave the room you would be blind.

I lust for her touch time after time.

I catch myself in a zone thinking of her again and again.

She is the type that a man will love in the beginning and in the end.

She is a very special person, but even a better friend.

If we go on a date I wouldn't let her spend a dime just because she is fine as red wine.

She is the type that I would cherish because she is a perfect person inside and out.

She is worth every minute of my time, and every hour because her love is like power.

My lust for her makes me want to rush and love her to the end just to start all over again.

In the hearts of men we pray for a love that will be with us to the end.

Relationships seem to last longer when to people start off as friends

She is like the wind when she walk pass giving me a cool breeze.

I catch myself imagining me on one knee popping the magnificent question.

I must confess my lust for her be having me walking around with no rest.

I don't stress because I am blessed, but without her love I be looking a mess.

The lust for her touch grooves me to an unknown beat.

She is sweet like a treat, brilliant and unique.

She put my mind at ease even when it is 100 degrees I still freeze.

I never meet a lady with so much high standers.

She has a high I Q but to beautiful to see through.

She is independent with the right attitude toward life.

She is smooth and cool with everything she does.

She is a walking blessing in a women's perfection.

I like the way she paste herself as if she was a model with class.

She looks like she is the perfect women for a man like me.

But then again she might be too good for me.

I know I am not a perfect man, but all I need is one chance is what I be saying.

The lust for her touch got me in a rush for her love.

If she was mines, I will give her what every women wants.

I will be humble, funny, sensitive and romantic like she is everything to me.

I will be gentle and supportive; I will look her in the eyes, and tell her she is beautiful.

I will tell her she completes me, and that God has made her just for me.

I will show her a side of me that no women expect.

I will lay down rules give her the tool to let her know that the men before me were fools for letting her go.

I just can't stop thinking how smooth and refreshing her voice is to me.

She has the kind of voice that will make a man fall for her not by choice.

Every time I look at her, I can see the pride in her pretty brown eyes.

I love that she knows who she is, and she nowhere she want to be.

I am so attracted to her that next to her is where I want to be.

She no how to take care of business with no question ask

She looks so humble that she leaves me speechless.

She is like a star that I see by far.

She is someone that makes you wish she knew who you were.

She turns heads when she walks the street.

She will make a married man forget he is married and he will cheat.

I lust to get her underneath my bed sheets.

Just for her attention she will make a man go out his way just to mess up his whole day.

I can't seem to understand why I have a strong sexual desire for this girl.

This is a girl that I would queen in my world.

The lust for her touch- I lust for her touch day after day.

At times I take a short brief look at her as she walks my way looking as beautiful as the day.

All I can say is hey and how is your day.

She stands about 5/5 with pretty brown eyes.

She has a smile that would turn a man's world upside down.

Her skin looks so smooth, chocolate and soft.

I know that she has a big heart because she is very smart and kind with an open mind.

In my mind I am thinking of ways to make her mine.

She be having me thinking things like what should I do are say to get her to come over my way.

She is like a brand new design; she is always on time and the first in line to be on my mind.

Sometimes I think she be giving me signs, but then again, I guess it is just her beauty messing with my mind.

I lust everything about her style, I think me and her will make a beautiful child.

She is tremendous in a way that I can't explain.

Miracle is her name and she is what every man want.

She is what every man wants to wake up to.

Her pride is what makes me want to just reach out my hand and do good thing for her because she deserve the best.

The lust for her touch- I lust for her touch 24/7

I smile when she speaks to me because she has class with no question ask.

But then again I might sound a little creepy, but I lust for her touch so deeply.

I am in love with her personality and the way she handle her business.

She is so independent and sweet like a treat that I seek.

Sometimes my mind wonder and I visualize us being together.

I can pitcher me and her together, but that is a dream that might never come true.

But just the thought of it makes my day better for the best and nothing less.

It's like when I think of her it wipe away all of my stress.

She is like a clinch to my thirst as I drink to the last drop.

From the first day I saw her I knew that she was one of a kind.

I said to myself, the things I would do if she was mines.

I wonder how I can get her on my line. But Wow! She is so fine.

She is Pretty, beautiful and kind, she the type of women that is hard to find.

My lust for her touch takes control of me and I am completely under her control.

She is top of the line to fine and my only wish is for her to be mines.

Every time she passes me by my eyes press rewind time after time.

This girl makes me change my ways because she is amazing with class.

But am I blinded by my feelings for her that got me so in lust for her touch.

I am in lust with her smile, she the type that makes a man feels proud.

She the type that makes a man thinks out loud.

She the type that makes a man gets on his knees and promises her the world, diamonds and pearls.

My lust for her takes over my mind as if I loved her over time.

I was taught to have patience and wait for love, but my heart is racing fasting then a plane flying above.

Is it my lust for her touch that got me close to the edge?

I mean I am a step away from falling in love from lust.

From dusk to dawn I lay in bed wishing she was in my arms.

Just imaging if it was a storm how I would hold her and keep her warm.

My lust for her touch gives me vibes that make me feel like I am inside her.

I fantasize us making love more than 3 times a day.

And every time the sex gets better and better.

She makes my night into day whenever she comes my way.

She makes me do different things, sweet things that make me sing.

For the girl of my dreams it seems as if I would do anything.

I lust for her touch and pretty smile that makes me say oh wow.

This girl got me stuck in a dream.

Trust me- she is someone you never seen.

It seems like I have seen all that I can see, and I have had everything, but her love that I lust for is so deeply.

This girl! This girl! Who is this girl that makes my heart sing?

I wonder will she complete me on this lustful road where love story are told.

My lust for her is deep even when I sleep.

She is so unique that my goal is to make her mines to keep.

I lust for her touch time after time, and it is amazing how this beautiful creature has taken over my mine.

True love is what I search for and I wonder will I find that in her.

She stands tall with her head on her shoulders, and I can only wish I was holding her in my arms on cold nights keeping her warm.

Her body will make the room glow and she handle her business like a pro and this I do no.

The intensity she brings in the room all too soon is a feeling of life great expectation.

My lust for her has gotten me out of control because I want to cherish her love like a pot of gold.

Together we will live young into we are old.

Being a man and being beside her you have to have self-control.

I lust for her touch on a raining day and I dream of her in a romantic way.

I speak beautiful words to get her attention on this mission for her love.

It is hard to find the perfect lady out here that will make you give her the world.

Every man dream of finding that perfect girl that will fulfill they every need.

The lust for her touch got me in a rush for her love

CHAPTER 12

3sum gone wrong

Like a sad song unknown it isn't nothing like a threesome gone wrong.

In a zone on my own trying to stay strong how could my threesome go wrong?

In the mist of my temptation I was eager to try something new. I was ready to get freaky with not just one girl but two.

Fun- fun- and more fun in bed lead to a mess of stress, are should I say trouble.

I had it all planed out- at least that's what I thought, but it happened unexpectedly.

I was chilling with my lady friend name Caramel who wanted to come over for some sex one night, but I had plans with another girl the same day.

I may have mentioned it to one of them about a 3sum and let the other one find out naturally are should I say unexpectedly.

So here I go with my lady friend Caramel over and we were chilling sexing and laying around the house. I get a call from my other lady friend name Candy asking me what's up.

She said she was coming through later on and told me to go by her a drink.

I'm saying to her ok, but not telling her that I had company already lying in my bed room.

I went and bought her a drink, which I got too bottles of ciroc because it was two different flyovers and I forgotten the kind that she liked to drink.

So Candy comes over and we sitting around talking for a little bit. I tell her that I have company in the back room. So I'm like I got my friend Caramel in the back room I forgot to tell you on the phone.

She says you should have been told me that you on some B.S. So she says tell her to leave. I told her that I picked her up and I got to take her home. Then I said don't worry about her she not gone trip.

So me and Caramel started drinking and talking and then we headed tothe other room.

I asked her was she down for a 3sum and she say boy please. We start kissing and then we took off our cloths then we started sexing.

After a while We go back into the living room;

I am sitting in the living room sipping more liquor and she jumps on me and start riding me on the couch and kissing on my neck getting me all wild and up.

I didn't want to leave my girl Caramel left out because she was down for whatever and I suppose to be giving her loving all day. So I say Candy let's go in the room and have a 3sum.

she is like no I never did that before. I just grabbed her and took her in the back room, threw her on the bed next to Caramel and started having sex with her.

She was into it squirting and feeling good so I got them both into freaking one another and the fun was happing. Thing was going down just as the night was getting to day.

It was over and we stopped because Candyl had to be at work the next day so she stepped out of the room. I and Caramel started doing it some more and Candy walked back in the room and said so this is what yawl going to be doing why I'm at work.

I smiled a little like what you mean. After that Candy just flipped out, she was loud upset about every little thing. I am saying to her cum down it's not that serous. So now I am trying to hold her and talk her into shutting up, but she never did and it was crazy.

Another 10 are 20 min pass by and my ex-girlfriend Lakeisha came over looking and laughing l saying what you got going on over here. I say nothing, but I don't know what's going on with her. {Candy}

So Candy starts talking to my ex girl friend Lakeisha telling her about me.

She said to her girl he a peace of crap and he isn't about nothing. No good! He's just a no good dog.

right away Candy gets to telling her my business.

So she said to her when yawl was together he was having sex with me, and I remember the day because he said yawl got into it.

She was telling everything. Then she said you came over and you were knocking on the door, I was in the house with him. That's why he never answered the door; he just let you pull off.

{Me I said} you can tell whatever you want because she already know, I told her everything so you can just zip it and go home and rest up.

Candy was was drunk and dang near out her mind because when I told her that she really got upset. She was throwing stuff around in the house just doing stuff to tip me off, but I'm keeping my cool and just trying to tell her to go home.

She wouldn't go home are shut her mouth so I'm like go in the room, and get some rest just call off work today and chill.

She like no shut up talking to me. She was really mad at me maybe because she just did something she never done before.

I took her in the room and tried talking to her. I get to kissing on her trying to apologize and be sweet.

All the sudden she just graved my TV and through it on the floor and it went boom.

So I say no way get out my house and go home. She wasn't hearing me at all like she was toasted and gone out her mind and I didn't know what was up.

We go in the living room and I'm trying to walk her out the house while she yelling in my face and I'm like come down. She graved my flat screen TV in the living room and tried to throw it on the floor.

Happily I caught it, but I was bout ready to grave her and throw her outside.

This girl was my sex buddy acting a whole mess and I am saying to myself omg.

The whole time Lakeisha is sitting right there cracking up laughing like she high are something. So Candy just walk back in the living room looking around like she trying to destroy something so she grabbed the counter in the living room with my glass cups and all in there and just pushed it against the wall. After that a fight broke out between me and her.

All glass broke and it was everywhere

After the tussling she went outside and called the police.

So the cops came by asking what happen and she tells her story and I tell mines. Then he ask my ex and Caramelwhat happen and they both told the cops she was tripping and she was gone out her mind, which she really was.

The police men sent her home and told her to let it go. Long story short I went in the house cleaned up the mess and slept for a few hours.

I get up to take my Caramel home then go to work and my truck had to flat tires so I'm like no way.

Lucky Lakeisha was still there because I had to take Carmel home. Instead she dropped her off then I went back to the house to think on what had just happend.

After about two weeks when I spoke to Candy again she said she doesn't remember anything because she was gone off an x pill. I was like wow you were really acting crazy.

I knew something was up because she acted a fool. If an x pill will have me acting like that I don't want it. lol

But still to this day Carmel still is my girl and I have a great love for her.

We had our little drama and still we messed around after that, but the 3sum was a night with fireworks in the sky.

What was supposed to be fun turned into a night with drama and negativity?

Like an unknown song you got to strong when a 3sum goes wrong.

CHAPTER 13

Single and loving it

Being single isn't everything, but is it everything that drama can't reach.

A lot of relationships landed me single because of all the fussing and fighting and that is not my style.

I like to keep my head clear so I can think properly.

I got a job to do every day and being single has provided me a better way to let my mind float.

I am a patient man who understands life, and the way we live it, but I'm single and loving it.

I know that time flies day and night living the single life.

Being single sometimes make me happy and I be so far away from being sad.

Everyone fill that it's a need to find someone to spend the rest of their life with, but not me because I'm single and loving it.

I wake up in the morning feeling younger in my mind, time after time.

I enter my day with a lot on my mind, but I still have nothing to say because I'm legit, single and loving it.

I got out of relationships just so I can focus on me, now I am single and doing me, feeling free like a bird in the tree.

I like to eat my cake and ice cream to and I will be doing that as long as the morning sky is blue.

I got girls that love me and I love them to, the ones that satisfy me I bless them gracefully.

People ask why I am single and I give them no clue.

I can call over a dip just to hit because I'm single, and loving it.

One night stands never are in my plans, but being the man that I am, I probably sex her like she is mind just so she can be on my line.

If she is fine with the right mind I might sex her in a slow grand time after time.

I know a lot of women get caught in their feeling, and they can be real destructive and that leads to ignorant.

Even if I am wrong, I am right because I'm single and all she wanted was the pipe.

I am pleased with myself, and I can love who I choose to love and sex who I want to sex because I am legit, single and loving it.

Being single has kept me active, sometimes I catch myself looking at ugly girls like they attractive.

After a long night of thinking and drinking then I am in my feelings.

I be hoping for someone to come home to, but I'm single and I got too much work to do.

What has my life come to where I stay out of relationship like they are only detractions to my accomplishments?

What could it be and why has my single mind accomplished so much that got me thinking I got the perfect touch.

At times I feel lonely, but then again I am drama free, single to be me and do what I want.

I can be a faithful man to a lovely lady daily, but I chose not to do because I'm in love with being single and doing what I want to do.

Maybe I am single for the right reasons and it helps my mind create.

I have no worries and no bathers just time and more time to do what's best for me.

Maybe I am just selfish and insecure for not being with someone I really adore.

I leave people wondering because I have some magnificent things in store.

Sometimes I feel like I'm ready to make that commitment then again I'm too legit, I'm single and loving it.

I am sent here to achieve something spectacular without being an actor, but I no love has a big factor in my life.

I know that I over think a lot, but I love my life. Maybe I am wrong for having multiple ladies in my life.

I have females friends that tell me you just a male tot. I say no I'm just single and I can screw who I want because I'm not commented to no one.

Then they say things like you just a big player you got all the girls, and I say that's a lie I'm just doing me watching time fly.

Just because I am single, it doesn't mean a thing. I still have my faith and my goals that are like dreams that only I have seen.

There is not one soul that can judge me for being me. The person I am, is the man I have grown to be.

When the time is right for me to settle down only I will know, and if the person I want has no interest in me so let it be.

Hey I'm single doing what's best for me like I'm in a world kid free.

When its game time and you have a lot on your mind, and there is no one to interfere with it, single and loving it.

When you got a nice chick on the side who is down for whatever, and you can't have no fun because you in a relationship ha-ha that's why I'm single and loving it.

Sometimes I rather be single then be a cheater.

I been in relationships that didn't last long, but it taught me things that helped me please the one that love me.

I learn things that helped me grow as a man without any plan in hand.

I am a faithful man inside, but that side I chose not to show.

I know that it's all about finding that special someone who understands you like you understand them.

I am single by choice, but whenever I hear that voice telling me it's time to settle down then my search will start for the girl who wants my heart.

But for now I am having fun like I'm on a mission to get the lady's sprung.

Sometimes my night be lit because I'm single and loving it.

I love who I am and I am proud to be the man that I am in a colorful world in and outside.

CHAPTER 14

Faithful colors

No matter what you do, and no matter what I may go through, I will always be faithful to you as long as the morning sky is blue.

You have been true to me sense day one, and I will be true to you to the end.

I can depend on you when I have no one else, and that's why I love you to death.

You are a cool breeze and a faithful friend yes indeed.

I am pleased that you are my boo, because I never fell in love with a lovely lady like you.

I will remain faithful to you on any giving day so I want you to trust in every word that I say.

I will be faithful to you to the end of time because there is nothing in this world that can get you off my mind.

My love for you is extraordinary, unusual but so remarkable.

I am faithful to you on a normal night because you shine bright and make everything alright.

Faithful Colors

A miracle you are to me, a beautiful creation that I see.

Through all my lovers I am always faithful to you in colors.

Don't listen to others who try to break up our beautiful colors.

Trust in me as I trust in you because it's our faithfulness that guides us through.

There are so many things that I love about you and here are two.

I love your smile and your sexy style that drives me wild.

You have a love that can't be replaced, and every night I can't wait to kiss all upon your beautiful face.

For your love I will race and I grantee that I will be in first place.

Have faith in me and I will forever give my love to you gracefully.

I listen so intently to the words you say so I can make you happy in the best way.

I love you for understanding me when I just wanted some space to find myself.

I was lost for a while, but I found all the love I needed in you and that is what got me through the cold and rough nights.

Being faithful to you is better than being right and that makes everything alright.

I love looking at you face to face because you are faithful to me in an extraordinary way.

I am thankful that I know what to do and say to keep a smile on your face.

At times it feels like our relationship is moving at a slow pace, but then again it moves in a faithful and safe way.

Being faithful to you has gotten me here with a mind to think and the eyes to see things clear.

I see you by far looking like a star, fresh as a brand new car.

My heart jumps whenever you are near. You are sincere and my goal is to keep you with me eternally.

I love you like no other, not only because we are lovers, but because we are faithful to one another.

There is nothing that can change my colors because I will love you forever.

When you are not around, I feel lost like I am waiting to be found.

When you are around I feel like I am on top of the world and it is upside down.

When you next to me, I am happy, silly like a clown.

When you leave me, I am sorry with a big face and a frown.

I love that you are down with me no matter the weather.

Whenever you need me just call and I will be there faster than ever.

You make my day better and I feel like I can love you forever.

I can never say never because I am covered in colors.

I am so faithful to you like a glass that no one can see through.

I am a faithful man and I only want to love you the best way that I can.

I want to make you feel like there is no other man.

Faithful Colors

I am so into you that I don't even understand.

The feelings you give me when I hear you tell people that I am your man is fascinating.

You give me a feeling that I can't explain, and that's why your love will forever remain in my heart.

I am blessed to be with you on this faithful mission into my own wishing.

I live my life doing what is right, but I don't make any moves without you in my plans.

It's my job to keep you stable so that you can do the things that satisfy you.

It is my job to keep you on your feet because you are the love of my life and that is just sweet.

I never thought that I would find someone who would meet the expectations and needs which I desire.

You like a fire that can't be touched because your love is just too much.

That's why I will remain faithful to you even when my time expires.

You are trustworthy, faithful, and sweet living underneath like a treat every man seek.

Sense day one I knew that you were going to be mines to keep.

There is nothing better than being faithful lovers.

Faithful lovers give birth to faithful colors.

You are the love of my life that makes everything right.

I am blessed to have you because your faithful heart makes my wishes come true.

The love of our colors gives us faith in our hearts that was there from the start.

You are one of a kind with a perfect mind.

My faithful ways has awaking me to brighter days.

It's good to wake up to the one who love you the most.

There is nothing better when you have a faithful lover because it is like no other.

Being faithful is a piece of mind that keeps your heart for the one person you love.

I am faithful in many ways, my life and future starts with colors loving one another.

Our hearts desire the most and together our love coast from here to there to the air.

I am a faithful man to my lovely lady, proud fully and gracefully.

My dear you have made me into a better man who understands that I am only a working man with a pin in my hand.

I give you my all because you do so much for me intensively.

You cared for me when no one else did, and that's why I will do whatever it take to make you happy.

You gave me pride when I didn't have faith in myself;

You gave me love when I didn't have anyone else to love.

You gave me confidence to keep doing what I am doing on this blurry road where story get told.

You turned my frown into a smile, and just to have you around has made me proud.

I am a faithful man in line for the number one prize, and the prize is to win your heart.

My heart coast as I toast to the one that I love the most and the one that loves me the most.

It is a sensational feeling to be loved by the one who loves you no matter what you do and no matter what you may be going through.

My faithful colors are a part of life.

My faith in love is real and it reveals as I live my life in colors.

Even through difficult times and days my sweetheart amazes me so briefly.

Sometimes I am funny but not often, when she next to me I am happy more than often.

I always try to be truthful to her morning, noon, and night.

Me being the man that I am, I try to understand the way women think when it comes to a relationship, intimacy, and love.

I am faithful to her because she is faithful to me. I love her because she loves me.

I do for her more than she would ever do for me.

I do for her more than I do for others simple because she is my everlasting lover.

My heart is pure because my love is real.

I have nothing but time and chance on my side because my faithful ways has awaking me to better and brighter days.

I am thankful to have a lovely and faithful lady on my side.

She is like my bread and butter.

This is why I love our faithful colors.

When there is no other, I turn to my lover and she sets my mind at ease because it's my need to please her intentionally and faithfully.

To be continue

www.ingramcontent.com/pod-product-compliance
Lightning Source LLC
LaVergne TN
LVHW091601060526
838200LV00036B/938